THIS IS ME! ACROSTICS

Poetry Stars

Edited By Roseanna Caswell

First published in Great Britain in 2022 by:

YoungWriters®
Est. 1991

Young Writers
Remus House
Coltsfoot Drive
Peterborough
PE2 9BF
Telephone: 01733 890066
Website: www.youngwriters.co.uk

All Rights Reserved
Book Design by Ashley Janson
© Copyright Contributors 2022
Softback ISBN 978-1-80459-029-4

Printed and bound in the UK by BookPrintingUK
Website: www.bookprintinguk.com
YB0507T

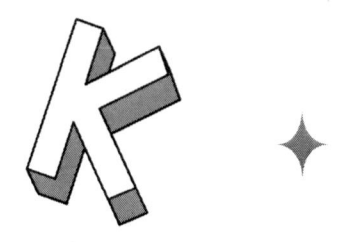

Foreword

Welcome Reader,

For Young Writers' latest competition *This Is Me Acrostics*, we asked primary school pupils to look inside themselves, to think about what makes them unique, and then write an acrostic poem about it! They rose to the challenge magnificently and the result is this fantastic collection of poems, celebrating them and the things that are important to them.

Here at Young Writers our aim is to encourage creativity in children and to inspire a love of the written word, so it's great to get such an amazing response, with some absolutely fantastic poems. It's important for children to focus on and celebrate themselves and this competition allowed them to write freely and honestly, celebrating what makes them great, expressing their hopes and fears, or simply writing about their favourite things. *This Is Me Acrostics* gave them the power of words.

I'd like to congratulate all the young poets in this anthology, I hope this inspires them to continue with their creative writing.

Contents

Independent Entries

Krish Kotecha (5)	1

Anderton Park Primary School, Sparkhill

Areeba Naeem (6)	2
Zeeshan Salam (7)	3
Amelia Jabeen (7)	4
Aairah Sheraz (6)	5
Hassan Hussain (6)	6
Tasnim Hammouti (6)	7
Kaamil Alum (6)	8
Eliza Islam (6)	9
Maliha Shaeed (7)	10
Umayr Tarafdar (6)	11
Omer Eldrieny (6)	12
Donia Najib (6)	13
Ayaan Arafat (7)	14
Zayan Mahmood (7)	15
Imaan Ahmed (7)	16
Essa Asghr (6)	17
Nura Osman (6)	18
Esa Hussain (7)	19

Cranbrook Primary School, Ilford

Brianna Valea (6)	20
Hafsa Ahmed (6)	21
Aryan Ahmed	22
Emaan Hashmi (6)	23
Ava Chong (6)	24
Ismaeel Pandor (6)	25
Ekampreet Kaur (5)	26
Aaira Hussain (5)	27

Khadeejah Okelola (5)	28
Victoria Alice Khatri (5)	29
Irina Jannat Hossain (6)	30
Mithiren Michael (6)	31
Sophia Alisha Islam (6)	32
George (6)	33
Eliza Abddin (6)	34
Macey Kavanagh (5)	35
Aadrithi Arrolla (6)	36
Aishah Shakeel (5)	37
Muhammad Fahar (5)	38
Tayiba Hussain (6)	39
Carolina Vazoi (6)	40
Nirvair Panam (5)	41
Aiesha Kumar (5)	42
Divam Bhalwal (6)	43
Rohail Mahal (5)	44
Ammara Paderwala (5)	45
Essam Shahid (6)	46
Zahra Akhtar (5)	47
Muhammad Ali Atiaf (5)	48
Aisha Zeb (5)	49

Greenside Primary School, Pudsey

Molly Dix (7) & Aubrey Dix (7)	50
Ella Hanson (7)	51
Esmai Rider (6)	52
Luciana Haigh Del Rio (5)	53
Taylor Adams (7)	54
Molly Dix (7)	55
Hemi Hughes (7)	56
Harrison Lowther (6)	57
Ocean Munro (5)	58
Rafaela Muqueba (6)	59

Grace Crompton (6)	60
Sophia Taylor (6)	61
Mollie Kitson (6)	62
Freddie Way (5)	63
Isobel James (6)	64
Arthur Welch (5)	65
Lola Fox (7)	66
Emily Sunter (5)	67
Teddy Sleaford (5)	68
Esther Cash (6)	69
Eddie Jones (7)	70
Casey Broadbent (5)	71
Lily Waite (7)	72
Noah Meegan (6)	73
Elliott Tallant (5)	74
Emma Cash (6)	75
Hareesh Dhiliwal (6)	76

Hallwood Park Primary School & Nursery, Runcorn

Frankie O'Neill (5)	77
Ebonie Jones (6)	78
Ashton Armstrong (6)	79
Brody Mills (6)	80
Layla Davies (6)	81

Our Lady & St Edward Primary & Nursery Catholic Voluntary Academy, Nottingham

Anjolaoluwa Omoesho (7)	82
Hanelle Bryan-Mayler (7)	83
Elijah Sylvester (7)	84
Cleondra Ubogu (6)	85
Thomas Skeoch (7)	86
Timileyin Atoyebi (6)	87
Isabella Withington (6)	88
Kian Hay (6)	89
Gabi Essien (6)	90
Dorian Koziun (6)	91
Orlaith Horan	92
Valerie Ugoh (6)	93

Penshurst CE Primary School, Penshurst

Barney O'Brine (5)	94
Chelsea Brink (6)	95
Zachary Subhan (6)	96
Bunnirose Ugo (5)	97
Matilda Abu-Moghli (6)	98
Oscar Wheeler (6)	99
Theodore Foster (7)	100
Indira Ergric (5)	101
Sophie Cain (7)	102
Zara Erglic (5)	103

Ryefield Primary School, Hillingdon

Penny Vincent (6)	104
Mason Jenkins (7)	105
Cameron Oberholster (7)	106
Maria Rohnean (6)	107
Esme Glaister (7)	108
Jordan Shepherd (6)	109
Bonnie Mason (7)	110
Liana Abedinzadeh (6)	111
Harley Russell (6)	112
Carly Antunes Coelho (7)	113
Humza Rehan Syed (6)	114
Emily McGee (7)	115
Kayden Dow (6)	116
Tilly-Ann Watkins-Ralph (7)	117
Sama Al-Tamimi (6)	118
Jacob Gardner (7)	119
James Withey (7)	120
Sania Ali (7)	121
Alex Onyshkiv (6)	122
Lily Urquhart (6)	123
Mia Raaczkowska-Czarnecka (7)	124
George Stout (6)	125
Honey Fifield (6)	126
Shaun Delaney (6)	127
Rome Richardson (7)	128

St John's Beaumont Preparatory School, Old Windsor

Aveer Puri (6)	129
Connor Hall (6)	130
Zachary Day (7)	131
Alejandro Gonzalez (5)	132
Tahaan Seebaruth (6)	133
Sebastian de Lange (7)	134
Evaan Singh Rajawat (6)	135
Noah Hutchinson-Lawson (6)	136
Xaviar Khan (6)	137
Harry Forsyth (5)	138
Thevin Pathmaperuma (6)	139

Thorpe Lea Primary School, Thorpe Lea

Violet Bedford (7)	140
Aryana Vidican (7)	141
Cecie Williamson (6)	142
Alex Rogan (6)	143
David Mcdonald (6)	144
Austin Edwards (7)	145
Afia (7)	146
Eleni-May Lynch (7)	147
Daniel (7)	148
Tegan Saunders (7)	149
Mystica Vinodaran (5)	150
Natalya-Marie Beldom (5)	151
Delilah Bedford (5)	152
Emilie Hammond (5)	153
Seher (5)	154
Alex Charles Lee (6)	155
Jai (6)	156
Jon Dickson-Diprose (6)	157

The Acrostics

Space

S pace is my favourite subject
P lanet X is a hypothetical planet
A steroid belt is between Mars and Jupiter
C eres is a dwarf planet
E arth is the third planet from the sun.

Krish Kotecha (5)

Areeba

A untie is my best friend
R ed is my favourite colour
E very day I go to school smiling
E very day I love to learn
B eaches are the best places
A wesome sisters around me.

Areeba Naeem (6)
Anderton Park Primary School, Sparkhill

Zeeshan

Z any and crazy
E very day, I play with toys
E veryone says I am adorable
S ometimes listen to music
H appy and kind
A lways on my iPad
N ever watch TV.

Zeeshan Salam (7)
Anderton Park Primary School, Sparkhill

Amelia

A lways happy
M y dad is brilliant
E very day help with the cooking
L ovely and friendly
I always wake up happy
A lways playing with my brother.

Amelia Jabeen (7)
Anderton Park Primary School, Sparkhill

Aairah

A lways there to help
A rt and drawing are my favourites
I like tigers
R eading is my favourite
A lways smiling
H elpful and great at cooking.

Aairah Sheraz (6)
Anderton Park Primary School, Sparkhill

Hassan

H appy to see my family
A nimals are my favourite
S miling and kind
S uper fast at running
A rt is my favourite
N ever gives up.

Hassan Hussain (6)
Anderton Park Primary School, Sparkhill

Tasnim

T hree big sisters
A lways happy
S chool is fun for me
N ice and kind
I ce cream is my favourite food
M y mom is strict but fun.

Tasnim Hammouti (6)
Anderton Park Primary School, Sparkhill

Kaamil

K ind and helpful
A mazing at running
A wesome footballer
M y favourite animal is a koala
I never break a deal
L ove my family.

Kaamil Alum (6)
Anderton Park Primary School, Sparkhill

Eliza

E very day I play in my garden
L ittle sister plays with me
I have for sisters and one brother
Z any intelligent
A rt is my favourite.

Eliza Islam (6)
Anderton Park Primary School, Sparkhill

Maliha

M usic is my favourite
A nimals are cute
L egoland is great
I ce cream is yummy
H appy and smiley is me
A lways being nice.

Maliha Shaeed (7)
Anderton Park Primary School, Sparkhill

Umayr

U nbelievable in art
M y favourite animal is a parrot
A lways happy and smiling
Y ummy is nice for me
R eady to learn.

Umayr Tarafdar (6)
Anderton Park Primary School, Sparkhill

Omer

O n my way to school always smiling
M y favourite animal is a snake
E very day, I play football
R eally great at sports.

Omer Eldrieny (6)
Anderton Park Primary School, Sparkhill

Donia

D oughnuts are my favourite
O nly have two sisters
N ever be sad
I love reading
A nimals are my favourite.

Donia Najib (6)
Anderton Park Primary School, Sparkhill

Ayaan

A lways happy
Y ummy chicken and chips
A mazing at writing
A cting smart all the time
N ever sad at all.

Ayaan Arafat (7)
Anderton Park Primary School, Sparkhill

Zayan

Z any and intelligent
A lways kind
Y ou can count on me
A lways walk to school
N ever mean to anyone.

Zayan Mahmood (7)
Anderton Park Primary School, Sparkhill

Imaan

I love school
M usic is my favourite
A lways helpful
A mazing at dancing
N ever gives up.

Imaan Ahmed (7)
Anderton Park Primary School, Sparkhill

Essa

E very day good at games
S miling all the time
S uper at games
A lways trying my best.

Essa Asghr (6)
Anderton Park Primary School, Sparkhill

Nura

N ever unkind
U nbelievable at dodgeball
R unning all the time
A rt is my favourite.

Nura Osman (6)
Anderton Park Primary School, Sparkhill

Esa

E very day, I play outside
S ometimes I go to the park
A lways learning.

Esa Hussain (7)
Anderton Park Primary School, Sparkhill

I'm Brianna

B alloons are pink
R un to the shop
I magination and creation
A fter shopping, I start cooking
N othing can stop me
N achos are my favourite chips
A nybody can deal with music

V egetables are on the table
A pples are clean
L ipstick is pink
E verybody is joyful with me
A ll are my best friends.

Brianna Valea (6)
Cranbrook Primary School, Ilford

The Rainbow

H ot days are the best
A pple in my hands
F antastic beach
S unshine I love
A pples I love

A art galleries I go to
H ouse, I went to my aunty's house
M ake cookies
E very day is fun
D ad is the best.

Hafsa Ahmed (6)
Cranbrook Primary School, Ilford

Roblox

R eliable Roblox, always working
O bbies are fun and hard
B ed Wars, the most action-packed game
L egendary game 'Adopt Me' is really popular
O bbies require time as there are 100 stages
e **X** treme games like Natural Disaster are about survival.

Aryan Ahmed
Cranbrook Primary School, Ilford

Teacher

T eachers teach us to read and write
E ncourages us and gives us stickers
A lways keeps us safe
C ares for us
H olds our hands when we are sad
E ven dances when we are glad
R eally loves us and is helpful to the class.

Emaan Hashmi (6)
Cranbrook Primary School, Ilford

Family

F riends are like family
A lso, my parents look after me and
M y family is special to me
I make them happy and make them laugh
L istening to my family is great
Y ou and me have a big family.

Ava Chong (6)
Cranbrook Primary School, Ilford

Ismaeel

I live with my family
S ara is my big sister's name
M aths, I love so much
A dam is the name of my dad
E njoying dinner together
E ating my favourite snack
L oving my family.

Ismaeel Pandor (6)
Cranbrook Primary School, Ilford

Barbie

B is for a beautiful, cute doll
A is for angel, living in the sky
R is for radiant and bright face
B is for bouquets of flowers
I is for imagination in mind
E is for an enjoyable life.

Ekampreet Kaur (5)
Cranbrook Primary School, Ilford

Funfair

F amily get together
U p and down on the rides
N ice and tasty candy
F riends with their families
A ll go round the merry-go-round
I nteresting games to play
R ides everywhere.

Aaira Hussain (5)
Cranbrook Primary School, Ilford

Spring

S pring, everyone plays
P laying in the sun in spring
R eady to play outside in the quiet
I like playing outside peacefully
N aming people their own names
G ood day, ready for summer.

Khadeejah Okelola (5)
Cranbrook Primary School, Ilford

Snowman

S pring or winter?
N an is making cakes.
O range is the scarf of Alberto.
W e love the snow
M um and I built a snowman
A lberto is his name.
N an is cutting the cake.

Victoria Alice Khatri (5)
Cranbrook Primary School, Ilford

Sister

S ister is the best friend in the world
I have a younger sister
S he is beautiful
T iny teeth look like pearls
E very day I play with her
R egularly we have dinner together.

Irina Jannat Hossain (6)
Cranbrook Primary School, Ilford

Football

F un to play
O ne point for me
O ver the goal
T eamwork is the best
B alls are round
A bility is good
L earn new skills
L ove to play with my friends.

Mithiren Michael (6)
Cranbrook Primary School, Ilford

Daddy

D ear Father, you are the best
A lways you help me to do my homework
D ay by day, you cook yummier food
D ecember is the month of your birthday
Y ou will get a nice gift from me.

Sophia Alisha Islam (6)
Cranbrook Primary School, Ilford

Roblox

R oblox is fun
O ld characters are cool
B ut the new ones are nice
L ately, I play a lot
O ther games I play less
X box makes Roblox fun.

George (6)
Cranbrook Primary School, Ilford

Summer

S o sunny
U nder the hot sun
M y mum took me to the beach
M y family had a fun time
E xtra fish and chips
R unning fast to the sea.

Eliza Abddin (6)
Cranbrook Primary School, Ilford

Summer

S unny today
U mbrellas are on the beach
M y birthday
M y holiday in the sun
E ating a picnic in the park
R unning on the beach.

Macey Kavanagh (5)
Cranbrook Primary School, Ilford

Winter

W inter is cold
I ce is slippery
N ow it's snowing
T he weather is very nice
E verything is freezing
R eally cold outside.

Aadrithi Arrolla (6)
Cranbrook Primary School, Ilford

Me, Myself And I

A mazing Aishah
I s intelligent and caring
S uper smart and cute
H appy and healthy
A dorable and active
H onest and helpful.

Aishah Shakeel (5)
Cranbrook Primary School, Ilford

Summer

S un shining brightly
U nder the heat
M any barbecue dinners
M akes people happy
E veryone loves the sun
R unning outside.

Muhammad Fahar (5)
Cranbrook Primary School, Ilford

Tayiba

T ime to play
A pples are fruit
Y ellow sunshine
I nformation is there
B irds are flying away
A mazing, nice people.

Tayiba Hussain (6)
Cranbrook Primary School, Ilford

Springtime

S un is bright
P lants are green
R ainy day
I n the park, I go
N ights are shorter
G oing outside every day.

Carolina Vazoi (6)
Cranbrook Primary School, Ilford

Happy

H aving fun with friends
A wesome family time
P laying outside
P acking for a holiday
Y ellow reminds me of the sun.

Nirvair Panam (5)
Cranbrook Primary School, Ilford

Castle

C at on a tree
A castle is red
S un is hot
T rees are green
L eaves are dry
E ggs are hiding.

Aiesha Kumar (5)
Cranbrook Primary School, Ilford

Football

F ocus
O pportune
O utstanding
T eam
B alanced
A thletic
L oyal
L ife.

Divam Bhalwal (6)
Cranbrook Primary School, Ilford

Mithu

M y best friend
I love him
T ogether we have fun
H e is funny
U nder the chair, he hides.

Rohail Mahal (5)
Cranbrook Primary School, Ilford

Teddy

T ell you secrets
E veryone loves it
D efinitely hug
D ance together
Y our best friend

Ammara Paderwala (5)
Cranbrook Primary School, Ilford

Candy

C ome and enjoy
A ll of us eat
N ice and sweet
D on't eat a lot
Y ummy and juicy.

Essam Shahid (6)
Cranbrook Primary School, Ilford

Mama

M y mama is kind
A lways helps when I get hurt
M y mama cooks well
A lways feeds me lovely food.

Zahra Akhtar (5)
Cranbrook Primary School, Ilford

Cooking Dinner

C ooking in the kitchen
O nions in the pan
O range juice in the cup
K ebab on the grill.

Muhammad Ali Atiaf (5)
Cranbrook Primary School, Ilford

Winter

W ind
I gloo
N orth
T ree
E gg
R oom.

Aisha Zeb (5)
Cranbrook Primary School, Ilford

Minecraft

M inecraft is the best game in the world
I n Minecraft, you can breed chickens
N o circles in Minecraft
E njoy playing it
C raft diamond pickaxes to mine obsidian
R abbits are fast in Minecraft
A lex is one of the most popular people in Minecraft
F ind the stronghold to defeat the ender dragon
T he best thing about Minecraft is you get to build cool stuff.

Molly Dix (7) & Aubrey Dix (7)
Greenside Primary School, Pudsey

Family

F amilies should love you and you should love your family
A family can be more than your relatives, it can be your friends too
M y family is important to me because they are kind
I n your heart, your family is always beside you
L ove will never leave you, it is always around
Y ou can't replace love.

Ella Hanson (7)
Greenside Primary School, Pudsey

Esmai's School

E very day I go to school
S chool makes me happy
M y school is fun
A place I want to be
I love school

R eading books at school
I s making me clever
D oing my homework
E arly mornings, however
R eady for another day at school.

Esmai Rider (6)
Greenside Primary School, Pudsey

All About Luciana

L ikes elephants
U nicorns are my favourite toys
C hinese, pizza and pasta are my favourite foods
I am from Spain
A lso, I want to be a teacher
N umber six will be my next birthday
A dam, Jo, Valentina and Sam are my family.

Luciana Haigh Del Rio (5)
Greenside Primary School, Pudsey

Florence

F anny was her mother
L eading nurses
O n the 12th of May, she was born
R e-wrote nursing books
E mbley Park is where she lived
N ursing soldiers
C rimean War
E veryone adored the lady with the lamp.

Taylor Adams (7)
Greenside Primary School, Pudsey

Happy

H aving a nice day with my family
A delicious, cold cookies and cream ice cream
P artying and fun make a good mix
P laydates with my friends make me happy
Y ou are great and responsible for your very own happiness.

Molly Dix (7)
Greenside Primary School, Pudsey

Friends

F riends are the best
R eally, they are the best
I love my friends
E ven when they make me sad
N ice friends are the best
D on't make me sad
S hall we play together happily?

Hemi Hughes (7)
Greenside Primary School, Pudsey

Swimming

S plash in the pool
W ater is cold
I wear a swimsuit
M ummy dunks me in
M e and my friends go
I wear armbands
N ext is the water slide
G etting out is cold.

Harrison Lowther (6)
Greenside Primary School, Pudsey

In The Ocean

O ctopus live under the sea
C oral is different colours
E mperor penguins slide on the ice
A ll the fish swim together
N arwhals are the unicorns under the sea, they are special like me.

Ocean Munro (5)
Greenside Primary School, Pudsey

Flowers

F lowers are pretty
L ovely colours
O ld leaves on the ground
W ind blowing away
E veryone loves to see flowers
R ain makes flowers grow
S un makes flowers bloom.

Rafaela Muqueba (6)
Greenside Primary School, Pudsey

Holiday

H igh balconies pointing to the sea
O cean has waves
L ook at a book
I ce cream melts in the sun
D iving into the sea
A t the splash pool
Y ellow birds flying.

Grace Crompton (6)
Greenside Primary School, Pudsey

The Princess And The Dog

S weet and sassy
O liver is my best cousin
P ink princess
H air is strawberry blonde
I ce cream is my favourite food
A Cavalier King Charles Spaniel is my favourite dog.

Sophia Taylor (6)
Greenside Primary School, Pudsey

My Fluffy Friend

H ugo is black and white
U nderstands my voice
G ood at miaowing
O ne of a kind

C ute and fluffy
A lways friendly
T o me, he is the best pet ever.

Mollie Kitson (6)
Greenside Primary School, Pudsey

Freddie

F ootball I love
R eally like Pokémon
E njoys swimming
D rawing is fun
D ance club keeps me busy
I nto WWE and Minecraft
E very day I do reading.

Freddie Way (5)
Greenside Primary School, Pudsey

Isobel

I am a good friend
S ometimes nervous about new things
O ne day, I want to be a vet
B londe hair, long and curly
E xcellent at being creative
L ike my family.

Isobel James (6)
Greenside Primary School, Pudsey

Arthur

A sks a lot of questions
R uns faster than a car
T akes swimming lessons
H as fun playing with friends
U nderstanding and helpful
R eads books to Mum and Dad.

Arthur Welch (5)
Greenside Primary School, Pudsey

We Are Family

F riends are fantastic
A nimals are awesome
M ummies are magnificent
I an was my papa
L ola? That's my name!
Y es, families are great.

Lola Fox (7)
Greenside Primary School, Pudsey

Teacher

T eaches us
E ncourages us
A dmires us
C ares for us
H olds our hand
E volves us into kind humans
R espects our efforts.

Emily Sunter (5)
Greenside Primary School, Pudsey

Teddy

T eddy is my name
E very day I like to play
D ominos is my favourite game
D addy and me dress the same
Y oghurt fills my belly every day.

Teddy Sleaford (5)
Greenside Primary School, Pudsey

I Love Rabbits

R unning around
A nd playing together
B ouncing up and down
B ut they get tired
I   n their little home
T hey snuggle together.

Esther Cash (6)
Greenside Primary School, Pudsey

Chewie

C hewie is my puppy
H e is mischievous
E very day, I play with him
W e love him
I give him treats
E xcited little puppy.

Eddie Jones (7)
Greenside Primary School, Pudsey

Casey

C ats are fluffy
A nd hedgehogs are spiky
S tars are sparkly at night
E xciting colours in the sky
Y ellow sun and white clouds.

Casey Broadbent (5)
Greenside Primary School, Pudsey

All About Me

L oves animals, especially pandas
I nterested in dancing and drawing
L ikes eating cheesy pizza
Y ellow is my favourite colour.

Lily Waite (7)
Greenside Primary School, Pudsey

Happy

H olidays in the sun
A fun time with Dad
P laying with friends
P assing a ball
Y ippee!

Noah Meegan (6)
Greenside Primary School, Pudsey

Me And My Cars

C ool car flips
A t my house
R ace on a track
S uper exciting.

Elliott Tallant (5)
Greenside Primary School, Pudsey

My Cat, Jess

C uddle my Jess
A nd sleep tight
T omorrow we will play.

Emma Cash (6)
Greenside Primary School, Pudsey

Cars

C ool
A ce
R ed
S peed.

Hareesh Dhiliwal (6)
Greenside Primary School, Pudsey

Frankie

F riendly and chatty
R eally helpful and loving
A ffectionate and caring
N ice to family
K ind to his friends
I maginative mind
E nthusiastic and hardworking.

Frankie O'Neill (5)
Hallwood Park Primary School & Nursery, Runcorn

Holiday

H ot, lovely weather
O ut in the ocean
L ollies and ices all day long
I nto the pool, I go
D ays out exploring
A fter dinner dancing
Y achts on the sea.

Ebonie Jones (6)
Hallwood Park Primary School & Nursery, Runcorn

Sonic

S uper fast, it's true
O nly hedgehog to be blue
N ice but has spikes
I ncredibly quick-witted
C ollecting rings with red shoes fitted.

Ashton Armstrong (6)
Hallwood Park Primary School & Nursery, Runcorn

Brody

B rody sees bees
R ed is my favourite colour
O range ice lollies are the best
D abbing in Fortnite is fun
Y ou need a friend like Brody.

Brody Mills (6)
Hallwood Park Primary School & Nursery, Runcorn

Layla

L oves to go to the park
A lways smiling
Y esterday, I had a party
L ove my mummy singing
A mazing.

Layla Davies (6)
Hallwood Park Primary School & Nursery, Runcorn

Friends

F orever make you happy
R eliable when you have a problem
I nclude you in their games
E at their lunch with you
N ever make you feel sad or upset
D ear to you and help you when in need
S hare their toys with you.

Anjolaoluwa Omoesho (7)
Our Lady & St Edward Primary & Nursery Catholic Voluntary Academy, Nottingham

Hanelle

H appy girl
A lways willing to help
N ever too shy and
E ager to learn new things
L ots of laughter
L oving and kind
E njoy the company of family and friends.

Hanelle Bryan-Mayler (7)
Our Lady & St Edward Primary & Nursery Catholic Voluntary Academy, Nottingham

Pikachu

P owerful electricity in his tail
I ncredible
K nocks out his opponents
A cute yellow animal
C ool
H uman owner named Ash Ketchum
U ses bolts of lightning.

Elijah Sylvester (7)
Our Lady & St Edward Primary & Nursery Catholic Voluntary Academy, Nottingham

Queen

Q uality in all her doings
U sually accepts people with warm arms
E verything she does is always on point
E ver beautiful
N ice in her style always.

Cleondra Ubogu (6)
Our Lady & St Edward Primary & Nursery Catholic Voluntary Academy, Nottingham

The Universe

S pace is dark and cold
P eople will float in space
A steroids move fast in space
C heese is not on the moon
E very star is a sun.

Thomas Skeoch (7)
Our Lady & St Edward Primary & Nursery Catholic Voluntary Academy, Nottingham

Pilot

P ilot in the aeroplane
I nside the cockpit
L ots of goodies to eat
O beying the flying rules
T o make our flight special.

Timileyin Atoyebi (6)
Our Lady & St Edward Primary & Nursery Catholic Voluntary Academy, Nottingham

Favourite Food

J ames is my daddy
A nd amazing cook
M y daddy makes great pancakes
E veryone loves them
S ometimes it is hot.

Isabella Withington (6)
Our Lady & St Edward Primary & Nursery Catholic Voluntary Academy, Nottingham

Wash

W ater washes lots of things
A sponge and some soap
S ome like it hot and some like it cold
H undreds of bubbles.

Kian Hay (6)
Our Lady & St Edward Primary & Nursery Catholic Voluntary Academy, Nottingham

Gabi

G reat at gymnastics
A mazing at recycling plastic
B rilliant at peek-a-boo
I am Gabi, nice to meet you!

Gabi Essien (6)
Our Lady & St Edward Primary & Nursery Catholic Voluntary Academy, Nottingham

Park

P eople are playing
A t the park
R unning so fast and
K icking the ball to score the goal.

Dorian Koziun (6)
Our Lady & St Edward Primary & Nursery Catholic Voluntary Academy, Nottingham

My Daddy

D oes silly things
A lways happy
D oes fixing
D ances good
Y es, I love him.

Orlaith Horan
Our Lady & St Edward Primary & Nursery Catholic Voluntary Academy, Nottingham

My Friend, Rose

R ose is my friend
A lso, my neighbour
T hat smiles a lot and
E veryone likes her.

Valerie Ugoh (6)
Our Lady & St Edward Primary & Nursery Catholic Voluntary Academy, Nottingham

Barney

B est friend to Coco and Bunnirose
A BC is a song I like to sing
R aptors and T-rex are my favourite dinosaurs
N ature makes me happy
E very day, I cuddle with Mummy
wh **Y** do we always to go to school?

Barney O'Brine (5)
Penshurst CE Primary School, Penshurst

Chelsea

C heeky Chelsea is my name
H appy running around
E very day, I dance at home
L aughing all the time
S miling at everyone
E njoying playing with my friends
A lways joking around.

Chelsea Brink (6)
Penshurst CE Primary School, Penshurst

Zachary

Z oos are my favourite
A lways likes being hot
C alm and a bit mad
H appy most of the time
A lways doing my homework
R eally good at maths
Y ummy yum yum, I love chocolate!

Zachary Subhan (6)
Penshurst CE Primary School, Penshurst

Bunnirose

B est friends forever
U nbelievable
N ice
N o strangers
I like being star of the week
R acing around
O ften happy
S omeone is kind
E asy to laugh.

Bunnirose Ugo (5)
Penshurst CE Primary School, Penshurst

Matilda

M agical Matilda
A lways outside
T all and amazing at singing
I s always laughing
L ove koalas and dogs
D aring horse rider
A pple of Mummy's eye.

Matilda Abu-Moghli (6)
Penshurst CE Primary School, Penshurst

Oscar

O utrageously funny
S uper at video games
C an't stop playing Power Rangers
A lways wrestling my brother and winning
R eally good at video games.

Oscar Wheeler (6)
Penshurst CE Primary School, Penshurst

Theo

T houghtful
H appy
E xtreme
O nly kind
D og
O nly helpful
R oses
E specially cool.

Theodore Foster (7)
Penshurst CE Primary School, Penshurst

Indira

I ce cream is my favourite pudding
N anny
D ogs
I s Zara my sister?
R abbits
A va is my best friend.

Indira Ergric (5)
Penshurst CE Primary School, Penshurst

Sophie

S weet stealer
O dd person
P arty lover
H i girl
I love being kind
E asy to laugh.

Sophie Cain (7)
Penshurst CE Primary School, Penshurst

Zara

Z oos are fun
A nimals are cute
R abbits hop
A lways smiling.

Zara Erglic (5)
Penshurst CE Primary School, Penshurst

Bright Home

B ig things
R ed things
I cy things
G reen things
H ot and cold
T o go home, stop tipping

H ome is everything
O ctopus loves to ink
M *oo!* is what a cow says
E ggs for breakfast from chickens.

Penny Vincent (6)
Ryefield Primary School, Hillingdon

Family

F amily, I spend time with a lot
A ctive all the time
M y daddy wants me to be successful in life
I 'll be kind to everyone
L illy is my favourite sister in the world
Y ou people, I take good care of my brother and other small children.

Mason Jenkins (7)
Ryefield Primary School, Hillingdon

Who I Am

C hristmas is my favourite
A t school, I like playing with my friends
M y favourite ice cream is vanilla
E xtra chatty
R on is my favourite school elf
O n the weekends, I feel free
N o one can stop me from sleeping.

Cameron Oberholster (7)
Ryefield Primary School, Hillingdon

Playful

P laying with my friend
L ending someone a toy
A nything makes me happy
Y ay! I love to go to school
F ull of love makes me happy
U nderstand everything in class
L ove is family.

Maria Rohnean (6)
Ryefield Primary School, Hillingdon

Energy

E sme has so much energy
N eighbours are my friends
E nergy is good
R ed is my sister's favourite colour
G arden are fun to play in
Y esterday, there was a child in my bedroom.

Esme Glaister (7)
Ryefield Primary School, Hillingdon

Jordan

J olly, fun and playful
O h, I'm always a good boy and a nice helpful friend
R un and play sports
D oing chores very fast
A sporty, football boy
N ow I have friends to make.

Jordan Shepherd (6)
Ryefield Primary School, Hillingdon

Bonnie

B unnies are my favourite animal
O ranges are my favourite
N ever naughty and I am nice
N o matter what, I am always smiling
I am nice to people
E lephants are my favourite.

Bonnie Mason (7)
Ryefield Primary School, Hillingdon

This Is Me

L ollipops are the best. I love them
I ce lollies are my favourite
A sporty, sporty pretty girl
N ice, helpful, kind and beautiful
A lex and Max are my friends, I like them.

Liana Abedinzadeh (6)
Ryefield Primary School, Hillingdon

Sharing And Caring

C aring is nice
A cat will warm your heart
R eally
I am happy when my mum and dad love me
N o matter what, I will always love you
G reat life with my family.

Harley Russell (6)
Ryefield Primary School, Hillingdon

Encanto

E nergy is me
N ewborns are so cute
C arly is my name
A lways happy
N ew clothes I love
T ea is my thing
O h, my brother is so funny.

Carly Antunes Coelho (7)
Ryefield Primary School, Hillingdon

Gold

H umza is like a gold hummingbird
U nder the shiny trees
M akes me brave because I like super shiny gold
Z ooming like a fast runner
A lways super speedy.

Humza Rehan Syed (6)
Ryefield Primary School, Hillingdon

Energy

E mily is full of energy
N ice and kind
E nergy is all you need
R un fast
G et sleep to get energy
Y ellow is my favourite colour.

Emily McGee (7)
Ryefield Primary School, Hillingdon

Sports

S port is my favourite
P lease throw it to me
O h right, you can join
R ight here
T he game has ended
S core in the goal.

Kayden Dow (6)
Ryefield Primary School, Hillingdon

Happy

H elping other people if they are sad
A mazing at gymnastics
P ositive and brave
P retty and kind
Y ellow, as sunny as the sun.

Tilly-Ann Watkins-Ralph (7)
Ryefield Primary School, Hillingdon

Elias

E lias makes me laugh.
L oves me because he cares about me.
I s cute and funny.
A messy boy who makes me laugh when he is being messy.
S o funny.

Sama Al-Tamimi (6)
Ryefield Primary School, Hillingdon

All About Me

J olly and kind
A lovely friend to Emerald Class
C ould play anything
O ctopuses are my favourite
B eing as kind as possible.

Jacob Gardner (7)
Ryefield Primary School, Hillingdon

This Is James

J ames likes jokes about chickens
A nd likes border terriers
M onkeys like him
E xtra amazing
S uper at writing.

James Withey (7)
Ryefield Primary School, Hillingdon

What I Dislike

S pooky crawly spider
P esky insects
I nsects
D umb bugs
E xtremely weird
R eally scary creatures.

Sania Ali (7)
Ryefield Primary School, Hillingdon

Alex Is So Happy

A sporty boy
L ikes cute happy dogs
E verybody wants to be my friend
X -ray for breaking my leg.

Alex Onyshkiv (6)
Ryefield Primary School, Hillingdon

Pink

P ink is the best
I like rainbows
N anny said I am beautiful
K ind I am.

Lily Urquhart (6)
Ryefield Primary School, Hillingdon

My Family

M y family make me happy
I am good at writing
A nimals make me happy.

Mia Raaczkowska-Czarnecka (7)
Ryefield Primary School, Hillingdon

Dogs

D igs dirt
O h so soft
G oofy and soppy.

George Stout (6)
Ryefield Primary School, Hillingdon

Dog

D og
O h so soft
G oofy and soppy.

Honey Fifield (6)
Ryefield Primary School, Hillingdon

Dog

D igs dirt
O h so soft
G ood dog.

Shaun Delaney (6)
Ryefield Primary School, Hillingdon

Dogs

D ogs dig
O h so soft
G uard dog.

Rome Richardson (7)
Ryefield Primary School, Hillingdon

Mo Salah, My Favourite Footballer

M o Salah, the best footballer in the world
O ne day, a thief robbed his house

S alah felt sorry for the poor homeless thief
A s he was very kind, he gave money to the poor man to build his life
L earnt to play football at the age of eight
A veer would like to meet him one day
H e is my great football hero and he inspires me to play football.

Aveer Puri (6)
St John's Beaumont Preparatory School, Old Windsor

Springtime

S pringtime is a fun time
P lants and flowers blooming
R eady to get outside
I love the bright blue sky
N ow it's my birthday
G et ready to party
T hen it will be Easter
I 'm going to get all the Easter eggs
M aybe you could join me?
E veryone come outside and play.

Connor Hall (6)
St John's Beaumont Preparatory School, Old Windsor

Zachary

Z ebras are my favourite animal
A rchie, Alex and Milo are my siblings
C hocolate ice cream is the best
H arry Potter is my favourite movie
A pples are yummy in my tummy
R unning across the football pitch I go
Y ay, it's my birthday on December the 11th.

Zachary Day (7)
St John's Beaumont Preparatory School, Old Windsor

This Is Ale

A lmost six years old
L ikes to play Roblox
E ats lots of pizza
J umps around the house
A nd sings and dances
N eeds to practise his violin
D oesn't eat peas
R eally loves Legoland
O h, it's great to be Ale!

Alejandro Gonzalez (5)
St John's Beaumont Preparatory School, Old Windsor

Mauritius

M emories of
A paradise of
U nspoilt nature
R elaxing by the beach
I sland in the sun
T asty food
I sland of natural resources
U nder the sun
S and, blue skies and sea.

Tahaan Seebaruth (6)
St John's Beaumont Preparatory School, Old Windsor

My Family

F amilies are the best
A lways having adventures
M y family is very kind
I n my family, we have lots of fun
L aughing and playing is great
Y our family is always there for you.

Sebastian de Lange (7)
St John's Beaumont Preparatory School, Old Windsor

Evaan

E very day I try my best
V ery happily create my Lego
A lways kind to all my friends
A t the end of the day, I love to see my family
N ever ever rude to anyone.

Evaan Singh Rajawat (6)
St John's Beaumont Preparatory School, Old Windsor

I Like Koalas

K oalas are my favourite animal
O n a tree they climb
A joey is a baby
L ove to eat eucalyptus leaves
A mummy has a pouch
S leeping in trees.

Noah Hutchinson-Lawson (6)
St John's Beaumont Preparatory School, Old Windsor

My Name

X aviar mean brave
A lways happy
V ery friendly
I love playing with Lego
A nd I know my dinosaurs
R eading books is my favourite too.

Xaviar Khan (6)
St John's Beaumont Preparatory School, Old Windsor

Lego

L ego is the best
E very day, I build something new
G oing through the pieces
O ver and over again.

Harry Forsyth (5)
St John's Beaumont Preparatory School, Old Windsor

Smile

S ays hello
M akes me feel excited
I am happy
L ike sunshine
E veryone loves it.

Thevin Pathmaperuma (6)
St John's Beaumont Preparatory School, Old Windsor

This Is Me

T horpe Lea is my school
H elping people when they are sad
I nto my playhouse, I go
S ometimes at the weekend, I get ice cream

I like to play on the beams
S pecial people eat good and rich food

M ornings when I get up, I hug my mum
E very weekend I go to gymnastics.

Violet Bedford (7)
Thorpe Lea Primary School, Thorpe Lea

This Is Me

T horpe Lea is where I learn
H earts and rainbows are everywhere
I f I'm sad, my mum hugs me
S he is so kind

I f I am too energised she asks me to go to bed
S he asks me if I want to eat something

M aria is my middle name
E very day I love to go on my tablet.

Aryana Vidican (7)
Thorpe Lea Primary School, Thorpe Lea

This Is Me

T horpe Lea is where I work
H aving a snack
I like wearing colours
S upporting football

I nterested in Lola's Room
S ometimes I go to my cousin's house

M y hobbies are ballet, football and karate
E xciting shows at the O2 with my mum.

Cecie Williamson (6)
Thorpe Lea Primary School, Thorpe Lea

This Is Me

T his Saturday, I'm going to the shop
H ugging is good
I like to do Lego
S ometimes I play hide-and-seek

I like playing
S ometimes I go to the shop

M y sister is special
E very Saturday, I go to the shop.

Alex Rogan (6)
Thorpe Lea Primary School, Thorpe Lea

This Is Me

T his is how I like myself
H ow I like my family
I am lucky to have myself
S pecial who I am

I love who I am and I love myself
S ometimes I have a special treat

M y family is the best
E very day I get bigger.

David Mcdonald (6)
Thorpe Lea Primary School, Thorpe Lea

This Is Me

T omorrow, I am going to my friend's house
H e is nice
I love my family
S ometimes we invite Ben

I am always doing something
S ticky toffee is nice

M y toys are big
E very weekend, I ride my motorbike.

Austin Edwards (7)
Thorpe Lea Primary School, Thorpe Lea

This Is Me

T his is marvellous me
H aving fun in school
I ce cream is good to eat
S isters make special friends

I am seven
S ometimes I like to eat pie

M y favourite colour is purple
E very day I watch Frozen.

Afia (7)
Thorpe Lea Primary School, Thorpe Lea

This Is Me

T horpe Lea is the best school
H elping my mummy
I love school
S ometimes I eat ice cream

I s she doing good work?
S omewhere I lost Bella Bear

M y mummy gives me cuddles
E leni likes ice cream.

Eleni-May Lynch (7)
Thorpe Lea Primary School, Thorpe Lea

This Is Me

T horpe Lea is my school
H ouse is the best
I s today Tuesday?
S nakes are creepy

I nsects and nature
S ometimes I laugh

M ental health is good
E verybody likes everybody.

Daniel (7)
Thorpe Lea Primary School, Thorpe Lea

This Is Me

T ime is going fast
H i everyone!
I like ice cream
S now baby

I t is fun going out
S mall is little

M y brother is the best
E very morning is tiring.

Tegan Saunders (7)
Thorpe Lea Primary School, Thorpe Lea

Mystica

M ystica loves cooking
Y ellow, I love
S uper friendly
T oo friendly
I eat lots of food
C an help
A t school.

Mystica Vinodaran (5)
Thorpe Lea Primary School, Thorpe Lea

Natalya

N atalya is kind
A lways
T oo nice
A lways happy
L ikes me
Y es, I am kind
A lways, I am kind.

Natalya-Marie Beldom (5)
Thorpe Lea Primary School, Thorpe Lea

Delilah

D elilah
E xcited
L ikes cake
I s joking
L ikes chocolate
A lways smiles
H elpful.

Delilah Bedford (5)
Thorpe Lea Primary School, Thorpe Lea

Emilie

E milie
M akes Lego
I s happy
L ikes surprises
I s excited
E very day.

Emilie Hammond (5)
Thorpe Lea Primary School, Thorpe Lea

Seher

S eher
E very day she is
H appy
E veryone likes her
R eally likes chocolate.

Seher (5)
Thorpe Lea Primary School, Thorpe Lea

Alex

A lways being me
L ikes football
E xcellent at maths
X -ray vision.

Alex Charles Lee (6)
Thorpe Lea Primary School, Thorpe Lea

Jai

J anuary is my birthday
A lways be kind
I s always helpful.

Jai (6)
Thorpe Lea Primary School, Thorpe Lea

Jon

J on is nice
O nly eats bananas
N o apples for him!

Jon Dickson-Diprose (6)
Thorpe Lea Primary School, Thorpe Lea

Young Writers Information

We hope you have enjoyed reading this book – and that you will continue to in the coming years.

If you're the parent or family member of an enthusiastic poet or story writer, do visit **www.youngwriters.co.uk/subscribe** and sign up to receive news, competitions, writing challenges and tips, activities and much, much more! There's lots to keep budding writers motivated!

If you would like to order further copies of this book, or any of our other titles, then please give us a call or order via your online account.

Young Writers
Remus House
Coltsfoot Drive
Peterborough
PE2 9BF
(01733) 890066
info@youngwriters.co.uk

Join in the conversation!
Tips, news, giveaways and much more!

YoungWritersUK   YoungWritersCW   youngwriterscw